LOOK BEFORE
YOU LEAP

LOOK BEFORE YOU LEAP

The Smart Author's Guide to Avoiding the Money Pit and Achieving Financial SUCCESS in Publishing

KATHRYN KEMP GUYLAY

Award-Winning and Bestselling Author

Author photo by Christina Carlson. Cover images used under license from Shutterstock.com

Published by Healthy Solutions of Sun Valley, LLC and Solu Publishing

This book may be purchased in bulk, with special discounts, for educational, business, organizational, or promotional use. For information, please email: kg@makewellnessfun.com

Library of Congress Control Number: 2017903134

ISBN-13: 978-0-9965328-7-7

To my now teenage children,

Elena and Alexander,

who always call me "a mom that works"

instead of a "working mom".

I love you.

SENDING YOU GRATITUDE

Thank you so much for buying this book. As an expression of my gratitude, I would like to offer you the Audiobook version for FREE!

TO DOWNLOAD:

www.makewellnessfun.com/LookBeforeYouLeapAudio

TABLE OF CONTENTS

INTRODUCTION

When I published my first book in 2015, I firmly placed two feet in a new world. This new place, what I'll refer to in this book as "the wild world of publishing," is one of the most bizarre and difficult industries I've ever navigated. My 25 years of experience in business, including working for a multinational corporation, a decade in management consulting, and another decade as the founder and executive director of a high-growth nonprofit, did not prepare me to write, distribute, and market a book.

I had no idea what I was getting myself into. I stood there with my fresh-off-the-press book, looking like a deer in the headlights with a stupid grin on my face. I was a published author!

Over the last two years, and through several more published books, that grin has been contorted into many expressions. But I have given up the wide-eyed Bambi look. No longer the frozen deer, I am now an experienced journeywoman who can navigate through the wild countryside with precision and finely-tuned senses.

I have immersed myself in author groups, participated in various mastermind sessions, attended and spoken at publishing industry conferences, presented onstage at the Book Expo of America, and conducted hundreds of interviews with authors and aspiring authors. I wanted to learn everything I could about the publishing industry so that I could protect myself—and later others—from some creepy stuff going on in the industry. That creepy diagnosis felt weird at first to me, the positive psychology lady who comes from a place of innate trust that all is well in the world and within people.

I have heard nightmare stories and even witnessed a few personal breakdowns. I have been angered by the deception to which some of my author friends have been subjected. I have slapped myself in the head when I have fallen for a stupid, money-draining trap myself.

Now, I have answered the call: "Kathryn, you understand numbers. Can you help me sort out this mess that is a stack of bills related to my book project?"

I have transformed that anger into motivation to help the many people who want to write a book but are in danger of running straight into the money pit.

Am I a 46-year-old Holden Caulfield, my favorite fictional character from my teenage years, who stands on a cliff to help the innocents? Maybe.

"Anyway, I keep picturing all these little kids playing some game in this big field of rye and all. Thousands of little kids, and nobody's around—nobody big, I mean—except me. And I'm standing on the edge of some crazy cliff. What I have to do, I have to catch everybody if they start to go over the cliff—I mean if they're running and they don't look where they're going I have to come out from somewhere and catch them. That's all I do all day. I'd just be the catcher in the rye and all. I know it's crazy, but that's the only thing I'd really like to be."

—J.D. Salinger, *The Catcher in the Rye*

Don't be a deer in the headlights. Don't fall off the cliff or get sucked into the money pit. Let me help you. Let me be your guide. Let me be the Catcher Before the Money Pit. Get your authorpower on, and let's get your book out to the world with a solid financial foundation and a firm smile on your face.

CHAPTER 1

Your Guide and Packing List

"If you would not be forgotten as soon as you are dead, either write something worth reading or do things worth writing."

~ **Benjamin Franklin**

THE ALLURE OF WRITING AND PUBLISHING A BOOK

Eighty percent of Americans report the desire to write and publish a book. With over 240 million adults in the United States, that's 200 million aspiring authors. That's A LOT of people!

I decided in college that I should write a book someday based on a quotation attributed to Jorge Luis Borges, the famous Argentine writer, although I'm not really sure that he said it. I have yet to find confirmation that these words came out of this mouth, but my favorite Latin American Studies teacher said them to me and essentially infected me with a nasty writer's bug that would incubate for many, many years. "If you want to leave a legacy and make any kind of ripple effect on the world, you must do three things: teach, have children, and write a book."

Teaching and having children became a reality for me in my 30s, but as I hit up against that dangerous midlife crisis in my mid-40s, I still had not figured out the book thing. Thoughts often haunted me in the middle of the night.

Was Ben Franklin harsh but right: Be forgotten as soon as you are dead? I'm going to die and be forgotten and let my favorite college professor down!

In 2013, I started reading books along the lines of *Publishing 101* and *Publishing for Dummies* and then moved on to some more sophisticated resources. I talked to my friends who had published books and annoyed them with my endless questions. I learned about agents, proposals, acquiring editors, and author groups. I watched the Will Ferrell movie "Elf," which portrayed a disturbing view of the children's book publishing industry. I was confused.

I also felt a bit like I was back in middle school. When I reached out to agents, acquiring editors, and anyone that I thought might lend me a helping hand, I felt snubbed. Why was I left out of inner circles, potentially being laughed at behind my back? I began to feel like a very unwanted stalker. I stood outside the party door of the mostly New York-based publishing industry, uninvited, as I imagined much merriment going on without me, connections being made, business cards being exchanged.

I left the closed door to the elite party and tried to erase the big scarlet letters spelling "Loser" branded on me. It was time for a pep talk, and what better location than right in front of my bathroom mirror.

Kathryn, you have an undergraduate degree from Emory with two majors and two minors. You have an MBA and significant work experience from your 20s and 30s in management consulting, putting together complex projects to cover strategy, goal setting, organization structure, job design, and incentive compensation. You have taken complex problems that companies such as IBM, AT&T, and Motorola could not figure out on their own and come up with awesome work plans and processes that led to the optimal answers. In your mid-30s, you founded and grew a successful nonprofit organization teaching health and wellness to tens of thousands of people. You hustled to get your Certification in Nutritional Counseling on top of your other degrees, and your efforts in the wellness movement were recognized by everyone from Alice Waters' Edible Schoolyard Project to Michelle Obama, with whom you dined at the White House. You have awards all over your desk and walls, from "Six Pillars of Character" to "Health Hero." You've got a radio show, a podcast, and a thriving coaching business for happiness, health, and productivity that your clients love. You sit on the board of several organizations, including an entrepreneurial incubator and accelerator that helps entrepreneurs start their businesses ...

Don't let those publishing people make you feel like a loser!

That pep talk took place in 2015. Along the way, I met more and more people who felt shunned by the publishing industry. So I gave them permission to give themselves their own pep talk and push on ahead. I'm happy to give you a pep talk, too. I don't care how you feather your own cap (with degrees, high-level experience ... or not!). Here's the key thing: NO ONE BUT YOU has had your life and your experiences and can tell your stories. Ultimately, writing and publishing are about telling and spreading stories. My pep talks aren't intended for people who want to bore everyone to death with bullet points of statistics and endless how-tos. Story telling is what engages the right side of our brain, our emotional brain, where we actually integrate and remember stuff. Statistics and dry information are immediately forgotten. So tell your stories, people. The world needs more inspiration.

BEWARE OF THE MONEY PIT

By 2014, I had the industry jargon down and, most importantly, knew what everyone was talking about when they said "PLAT-

FORM!" (more on that in the next chapter). I decided by 2015 that I would step into the very empowering title of "Author of the upcoming book ..."

Up front, it is important that you figure out whether you want to be a nonfiction writer or a fiction writer, as crossing between the two is a difficult endeavor. As for me, I know that I didn't have it in me to write about vampire hottie lovers or child magicians riding unicorns, so I made myself firmly at home in the nonfiction world. There are wonderful organizations for writers of both fiction and nonfiction, and I joined the Nonfiction Writers Association, led by the lovely Stephanie Chandler.

Nonfiction writing is all about establishing and leveraging your expertise, and I knew that I wanted to combine my decade of management consulting expertise with my decade in wellness consulting and facilitation, so I found my home in the world of "self-help." At first, I recoiled at the thought of being in the group of people that, as Stuart Smalley of the Saturday Night Live skit would describe in his *Daily Affirmations*: "I'm good enough, I'm smart enough, and doggone it, people like me!"

But self-help is a broad and important subject, and it includes so many of my favorite books, including everything by Jack Canfield and Marci Shimoff to *You Are a Bad Ass* by Jen Sincero. I figured I could fit right in with my authentic desire to help people. I started by outlining my first book based on positive psychology in the workplace and wrote the required proposal (after reading stacks of books with titles closely related to "How to Write a Book Proposal"). At first, I blushed at the offers coming in the door from publishers. But my blush quickly turned to burning red hot mad face. Weren't these offers to publish my book supposed to pay me for all of my hard work? I had an offer from one of the most prestigious publishers in the industry; as I flipped through the pages and pages of jargon, I realized they wanted me to *pay them* to be my publisher.

The wake-up call wasn't a nice little ding or chime. It was a rude HONK HONK HONK that sent me running off to the nearest and best intellectual property lawyer I could find. I still thank my lucky stars for finding Brad. Our conversations sent me on my own journey to figure out why the publishing industry is very much a wild world. You must be prepared and equipped before you jump in.

Since my awakening in 2015, I buckled down and carefully applied my management consulting experience to the world of publishing. I ran the industry through basic microeconomic theory, the Porter Analysis (I get made fun of for using this analysis, but I like it, so too bad) and basic venture capital models. I wandered the halls of the Book Expo of America in 2016 and saw some pretty desperate people. I scratched my head in confusion, drank bottles of wine to numb the shock of the real numbers involved, and wondered how this industry can possibly survive.

It ain't a pretty field of roses.

It's more like a big, ugly money pit. And 200 million people in the U.S. alone might be about to jump in?

Yikes.

The coach, mentor, and bleeding heart nonprofit founder within me jumped out and said: *"You! Yes, you Kathryn Kemp Guylay. Help these people!"*

I WILL BE YOUR GUIDE

So here I am, red hot mad face transformed to furrowed brows of determination, hoping to help YOU.

I know it is scary to think about putting yourself out there, which is what you do when you write a book and send it out into the world. When my first book, *Mountain Mantras: Wellness and Life Lessons,* was published (self-published, right in that self-help category that made me feel just a little anxious), I felt like I was running around the streets naked.

There are times, dear author, when you might feel naked as you move forward in your publishing journey. Here are the two ways I plan to help. I will:

1. Allow you to overcome your own objections to writing and publishing a book, and
2. Arm you with essential gear that makes sure that you don't sink into the scary money pit of publishing or get eaten alive by the strange, evolving beings that inhabit this wild world.

I'm going to take care of number one right here and now. Number two is really the rest of the book, so hang in there.

OVERCOMING THE TOP THREE OBJECTIONS TO WRITING AND PUBLISHING

Objection #1: I don't have the experience or expertise to write and publish a book.

My boot in your rear: Take time to seriously incorporate this saying into your consciousness: "There is nothing new under the sun." Yep, your fresh and new idea is not fresh and new. But if someone has explored that idea in the past, that means that your idea is actually a good idea.

In my yoga class, our teacher often plays this wonderful song called "Everybody's Free to Wear Sunscreen" by Baz Luhrmann. The lyrics are based on an essay written as a hypothetical commencement speech by *Chicago Tribune* columnist Mary Schmich (originally published in June 1997). The essay gives various pieces of advice on how to live a happier life and avoid common frustrations; it was often erroneously attributed to a commencement speech given by author Kurt Vonnegut at MIT. Whatever the background and pedigree are, here is how it goes:

> *"Advice is a form of nostalgia. Dispensing it is a way of fishing the past from the disposal, wiping it off, painting over the ugly parts, and recycling it for more than it's worth."*

In other words, your idea can be viewed as a fresh new product with an enticing new label that just might reach a new audience. Yes, even if that advice has been given before. Based on your unique life experiences, it is YOUR responsibility to create a new label for that time-tested advice and make it attractive to a new consumer. Guess what ... they might just never pick up that product unless they see the new label. So, if your ideas, lessons, and stories have value, even if they have been shared before, it is your responsibility to get them into the hands of people that need them. Make this world a better place.

Objection #2: I don't have the time to write and publish a book.

My boot in your rear: Okay, I'll admit that I have friends that have been working on a book for nine years. As you'll learn in the chapters to come, you can get your message out in a matter of months, if not days. I am not a fan of "write your book in one weekend" because creativity needs some time and space. You will need patience to formulate your thoughts. But you can write and publish in a *reasonable* amount of time.

For those who are still saying, "I don't have a minute to spare!" I'd like to ask you to take the word "busy" out of your vocabulary and replace it with "I'm not able to make it a top priority." We all have the same amount of time in our lives. Busy is not an excuse. I also know from personal experience that your book can be done in a matter of weekends within a 100-day period. I'm a fan of John Lee Dumas' *Freedom Journal*, and many people have used the combination of gratitude, intention setting, and focus to bring their books to life in a shorter amount of time than you might think possible.

Objection #3: I'm scared!

My boot in your rear: Yeah, whatever. I told you that the publishing industry is a wild world. Writing and publishing a book are not an activity I'd categorize in the easy zone. But haven't you heard that all of the growth in your life happens in the uncomfortable zone? So put yourself in that uncomfortable zone and GROW. I love advice I've heard from Tim Ferriss that I will paraphrase here:

> *"Do projects not because of the outcome but because of what you will learn during the process."*

You will learn a ton about both your inner and outer worlds when you write. In fact, one of my favorite power writing phrases is something I have heard Michael Hyatt say, but I believe it is attributed to Dawson Trotman:

> *Thoughts disentangle themselves when they pass through the lips and fingertips.*

In other words, write because it will help you to think more clearly about the things that are most important to you.

ESSENTIAL GEAR FOR YOUR JOURNEY

Now it is time to gear up for your trip into the wild world of publishing. You will need whatever organizational tools you like for scheduling your time and, of course, the basics like a computer or notebook (or even a recording device) where you will actually record your words. What I'm focusing on here are not the tactical writing and publishing items but the essential *survival* items. I've limited it to four items, as I don't want to weigh you down. I also don't want you to have so many survival items that you can't remember what to use when. Believe me, you will need them.

I won't be using the well-worn parachute metaphor. This book is called *Look Before You Leap*, but you might just have to bend your knees and take the impact of landing as gracefully as you can. Sorry, no parachute or even soft landing mattress pad made it on my list.

The packing list:

1. Map
2. Bug spray
3. Species guide
4. Compass

Let's go! It's time to learn the Four Agreements that are your map to navigating the wild world of publishing.

CHAPTER 2

Enter The Twilight Zone

"This highway leads to the shadowy tip of reality: You're on a through route to the land of the different, the bizarre, the unexplainable ... Go as far as you like on this road. Its limits are only those of mind itself. Ladies and Gentlemen, you're entering the wondrous dimension of imagination ... Next stop: The Twilight Zone."

~ **Rod Serling**

YOUR MAP CONSISTS OF FOUR AGREEMENTS

Are you ready for your first piece of essential survival gear? It comes in the form of four agreements that you will make with yourself. These agreements do not have anything to do with Don Miguel Ruiz's excellent book, *The Four*

Agreements. I wish they did. These four agreements mostly apply to authors working with traditional and hybrid publishers; I'll explain the differences between those two in the next chapter. Even self-published authors are exposed to some of the overall dynamics and the painful reality of the fourth agreement. So you might also want to get your bug spray ready!

Agreement #1: I am OK with the fact that products in this industry are sold to industry partners without them "seeing the inside."

A lot of my friends were really excited when I told them that I was an "author to be," after getting a few offers from publishers. The integrity of these offers, by the way, did not stand up to the test of time, but that is another story yet to come. I even went so far as to create a title, design a cover, and have the publisher create a one-pager about the book that one of the firms presented to the "trade"—the wholesaler in the industry, Ingram—that pretty much owns the distribution channel to every bookstore out there.

The conversations I had with my friends—let's take Annie, for example—went something like this:

"Wow, Kathryn. When did you have the time to write a book!"

"I didn't write it yet."

"But you just said that your book was presented to the biggest bookstore influencer in the industry?"

"Yes. It was pretty mysterious, but all the publisher wanted from me was a title, cover, information about my background, and information about my newsletter, social media, and connections."

"But what about the book?"

"I'll write it later, I guess."

In the publishing industry, you don't write your book and then approach a publisher to ask to have it distributed through the channels to get to bookstores. You'll learn more about how different publishers, or species, work in the next chapter, but I'll tell you now that books are sold in the industry based only on a proposal and maybe a sample chapter at most. Now, let's imagine that reality of the wild world of publishing applied to another industry, say real estate. In this next conversation, I'll play the real estate agent, and my friend, Paul, is a potential buyer of a house I'm listing.

"Kathryn, you're listing that great house at 1022 Perfect Lane that I've always wanted to buy. I've dreamed about living on Perfect Lane my entire life!"

"Great! The owners are really motivated to sell that place."

"I'm so excited. When can we take a look?"

"Sorry. The way I'm working these days is that I don't actually take anyone through a house. No interior views. Very few inside details. More of an outline and a couple pictures of the outside."

"Are you kidding?"

"Not kidding at all. You can just take a look at the proposal—here it is. It shows the exterior in full color! It then describes the rest of the house in terms of what might be there. I could probably take you in to see one room, but that's it. Then you make me an offer. Getting inside the house? That's for after you buy it."

Agreement #2: I will accept 100% of all returns, even after people have used and abused my product for an entire year.

I believe in return policies, and with so many people putting up online courses, for instance, which may or may not be any good, a 100% return, no questions asked policy has its place in our current economy. But online courses are not physical products and do not involve wear and tear, shipping, and significant costs that the content creator must pay. Let's look at a recent conversation between me and my husband, Jeff, that happened when opening the mail.

"Hey, Kathryn, you got something from your book distributor!"

"Cool! I need a cash infusion right now to fund something else I have going on in my business. I hope I sold a bunch of books this month and it's a nice big, fat check."

"Um ... you actually OWE them money."

"What!? But didn't I sell a bunch of books this month? I ran a bunch of promotions and did a ton of radio interviews!"

"Yes, but one of the channels—the wholesaler that sells mostly to libraries—returned a ton of your books that they bought a long time ago. I see shipping charges, handling charges, restocking fees. You actually have a really big amount that you owe your distributor."

"But didn't that wholesaler buy them almost a year ago!?"

"Yes, but they can return them. It's part of the contract. The books will be all beat up. I doubt you can resell them. There is an option here for you to pay your distributor to have your books destroyed."

"Whaaaattt!!!???"

I ran off to bury my head under a pillow and cry.

Now, let's imagine that reality of the wild world of publishing applied to another industry. This time, I'll be the person who bought a car from the Mercedes dealer. I'm in the mood for some luxury after my crying session. Jeff will be the car dealer. Sorry, Jeff, I can only take so much sharing of pain on a few pages; it's your literary turn.

"Hi Jeff. I've decided that I really don't like my car after all. I want all of my money back."

"Um, you've had that car for nearly a year!"

"Yes, I just don't have space for it in my garage. I just bought some new cars from some other dealers. So I want a full refund."

"But there are scratches all over the exterior! And in a few places you ripped the seat covers!!"

"Yes, I know. Maybe you can still resell it. Or maybe just destroy it. And I'd like for you to come pick it up at my house, actually. I need to get back home. You should be able to cover the transportation of getting this beat-up car back here, right? I remember that being in the contract."

"Whaaaattt!!!???"

Jeff runs to the back of the car dealership to put his fist through the drywall.

In case you think that this scenario is ridiculous, know that returns in the book publishing and distribution industry are 30% to 40%. Returning books is not just a problem for printed books. It is an issue for ebooks as well. You'll see below under Agreement #4 just how weird people can get about returning ebooks.

Agreement #3: I don't need to get paid right away, really!

When I was looking around to change distributors for my books, I called a fellow publisher who had been using my distributor but switched. Here is what his email said:

"Overall, I am glad I made the switch from (Distributor A) to (Distributor B) and would do it again. But there are certain pluses and minuses that make a one-size-fits-all solution elusive. I have found distribution to be the most complex issue we face as micro- or self-publishers."

When I called him to talk, it turns out that (Distributor A) was holding back six months of earnings, a third of the cash that he earned from selling books through the channels. They were holding his money even though he already earned it—he paid an upfront fee for distribution services, he paid to get the books ready, he paid to ship them to the distributor, and the distributor filled actual orders through the channels (and got their money).

Now, let's imagine that reality of the wild world of publishing applied to another industry, say my current coaching/consulting business. In this next conversation, I'm back to banging my head again as the service provider. My friend, Tracy, is the client.

"Wow, what a great staff retreat you managed for us. Thank you for doing all the prep work, showing up, providing a ton of value, and exceeding the expectations of the participant group. You did a fantastic job for us!"

"You're so welcome. We agreed the project total for the work would be $4,000. I've given my invoice to the accounting department."

"Actually, we are going to pay you just $2,700 now, just in case any of the participants has a minor complaint. We might need to deduct some from your final invoice, so let's hold off. I guess you should expect the remaining $1,300 that you've already earned in say, six months, if you get it at all. That's just how we do business."

"Okay ..."

I get into my car and bang my head on the steering wheel until the car honks and my head hurts even more than it already does.

If you do get paid, dear author, please don't set your sights on having your book writing career pay your bills for the rest of your life, unless your only bills are paying for camping sites to put up your tent while you go hunt for your own food. Later, I am going show you the raw, inside scoop on the financial situations of dozens of real authors. I did not interview John Grisham or Elizabeth Gilbert, as I don't think that basing results on examples that are several standard deviations outside of the normal bell curve will really help you. Perhaps you'll get really lucky, or perhaps you're a celebrity or were born with a special lucky constellation over your head. Then, you might be able to rake in the bucks and quit your day job. Or perhaps you are one of those folks that can just churn out material (especially in fiction, where readers are more voracious) and make a pretty darn good living just like the guys who lay out this model in the book *Write. Publish. Repeat.* I'm not saying you can't make money in writing and publishing. But if you are like most of the dozens of authors that I interviewed and hundreds that I've talked to, book writing tends to be less lucrative than working at McDonald's, once you consider all the costs—including your time—that you will invest.

Write because you love it, not because you will make money at it.

Agreement #4: I am willing to expose myself to ridicule daily.

In the publishing world, having a book without any reviews is a recipe for no sales. We are herd animals, so we need social proof before we try anything, but getting your book reviewed in the *New York Times Book Review* is something you might wish for in the way you wish to win the lottery. So authors look for options such as Netgalley (pricey), paid reviews (also pricey; Kirkus and other paid reviews run around $500 each), or they beg their friends and family to put reviews on Amazon and Goodreads. Family reviews are really not allowed on Amazon, by the way, and, if your friends are too closely connected to you, Amazon will take down the review. I heard a story that Amazon took down a review that an author's virtual assistant had put up because it made the connection. Crazy, isn't it?

So it's time to really put yourself out there to the larger public. Dear author, it is now time to pull out your next piece of essential survival gear: your Bug Spray. Hopefully your bug spray can keep away the pests and shield you from the inevitable ridicule you'll endure from some thankless readers.

We are living in times where we have traffic jams and frustrating situations around every bend, and people love to take it out on other people. Authors are an easy target. As I write this, *The Great Gatsby* has received over 300 one-star reviews on Amazon. A few samples:

"Total s**t, be warned."

"It's even more boring than that thing of Steinbeck's 'Of Mice and Men.' Avoid it like the plague. No. On second thought, get the plague, you'll be out of your misery earlier."

"The secret is: the author was a drunk."

"MAKES ABSOLUTELY NO SENSE WHATSOEVER."

And since I've already mentioned the *Four Agreements,* which I LOVE, I looked that one up on Amazon, and it had over 200 one-star reviews. Here is an example:

"This book is too simplistic, repetitive, and boring. I really wanted to like it, since the 'four agreements' on the description made some sense, but boy, the writing is so bad and the approach so superficial that I just couldn't bear it. The tone is somewhat preachy, too, which makes me wonder why the author isn't himself following his first 'agreement' and being more impeccable with his word."

I remind you, dear author, that the people who wrote these reviews probably paid $10 or less for the book, the price of a couple cups of premium coffee, yet consumers seem to expect the world from this cash outlay. Readers can be so frugal about their book-related expenses that they go to great lengths *to get their money back,* a la:

"I drank all three of these lattes and decided I didn't like them. Gimme my money back!"

The following post was recently on an Amazon discussion board. It was, not surprisingly, taken down the last time I checked (through an act of grace?), but you can still find it on the Internet if you'd like to search:

"I find it very unfair of authors to release part of a story. You would not buy half a burger if you wanted the whole burger. I can understand giving a few chapters for free (sample) so that the reader can see if she likes the story, and if so, buy the book ... I often cannot remember the parts already read by the time the next book is published. I find it unfair that the authors take advantage of the readers in this way. My solution to this is to buy the next book, read it, then return it for a refund. After about a year Amazon blocks the return for refund option. I then simply open another account ...

I suggest other readers start using their buying power to show authors we are not satisfied with this treatment. Hopefully at some stage authors will realize that their clients deserve better treatment."

You have my permission: BUG SPRAY at FULL force. Bug infestation is wreaking havoc!

I have one more great bug story, and this time it's personal.

I had heard that doing a Goodreads giveaway was a great idea for building awareness and getting reviews for one's book, so I did a few Goodreads giveaways for my second book, a picture book for children called *Give It a Go, Eat a Rainbow*. The charming idea behind the book, I thought, as did most people, is that it combines simple illustrations by my 12-year old son, Alexander, with real-life photography to create an augmented reality. The simple characters were designed to immediately draw kids into the story, and the real photography of colorful fruits and veggies was designed to provide kids with exposure to healthy foods. Targeting early childhood and elementary school children, this picture book promotes healthy eating habits.

Give It a Go, Eat a Rainbow is a 54-page, full color hardback book that retails at $20, and the shipping costs are another $5. So a Goodreads giveaway for just one person is a $25 gift from me as an author to a stranger. Here is one review I received after sending such a gift.

From Nicole, Goodreads reader, born on June 18, who, from her profile, looks to be in her twenties or thirties:

"I won this book in a Goodreads giveaway and would not have read it otherwise. Most of the colourful photo pages are great, but the drawings look like a child did them, and the book reads like a stoner's guide to nutrition."

I'll let you, dear reader, have your own reaction while I'll keep mine to myself. I do wonder why she is asking for free picture books for children if she is an adult who wouldn't normally read them? She must have been so uninterested that she didn't read the summary of the book inside the front cover that clearly states that the illustrations ARE by a child. That's the point! The stoner part just made me laugh...sort of.

In Nicole's honor, we spray an extra dose of bug spray every June 18 into the air and celebrate all of the positive reviews that other readers have given us. At this time, the book has an average 4.33 out of five-star rating on Goodreads and has 108 reviews on Amazon, with 91% of those being five-star reviews. Sadly because of my Nicole experience, I will never do another Goodreads giveaway again. Or so I say today.

As you integrate this final agreement—*I am willing to expose myself to ridicule daily*—know that the more popular your work becomes, the more prepared you should be to encounter bugs like Nicole. As I mentioned above, they are multiplying.

Now that you have a map of the wild world of publishing and have tested your bug spray, let's move on to a species guide so that you are better equipped to distinguish the various (and sometimes strange) beings that inhabit it.

While doing research on this project/book, I discovered an interesting way to get around each and every one of these four agreements, which I'd love for you to discover if you want to pursue a creative life but don't want to undergo the pain I've outlined. For more information please visit: www.makewellnessfun.com/nothanksagreements

CHAPTER 3

Species Guide

"Poets, priests, and politicians
Have words to thank for their positions"

~ **The Police**

It is important to understand the species that exist in this wild word of publishing, including traditional publishers, self-publishers, and hybrid publishers.

In the last chapter, I talked about how I wrote a book proposal and a sample chapter and then went looking for an agent or a publisher to help me bring my book to life. Since I had so much time with no one returning my calls, I decided to learn a little about what has been going on in the industry itself. Here are a few things I learned.

Way back in the 1960s, the publishing industry was mainly comprised of companies whose only business was publishing books. Then corporations started buying up the publishing houses and independent bookstores. When the big box retailers entered the market and created more competition, the publishing corporations became more risk averse and narrowed the type and scope of books that they published. They also started gobbling each other up to survive, until there are now just a handful of traditional New York publishing houses. They include Penguin Random House, Hachette Book Group, HarperCollins Publishers, and Simon & Schuster.

TRADITIONAL PUBLISHERS

Traditional publishers generally stick with known authors, celebrities, and past success formulas. Because these large companies are risk averse and elitist, they really do not like aspiring authors knocking on their doors uninvited. Traditional publishers rely on agents to make connections between authors and publishers, a type of filter. In order to get through the door of a traditional publisher, you generally need to have an agent. Or you need to be a celebrity and have access to anyone you possibly want to contact, including Oprah, the President, or Jimmy Fallon.

A note about agents: I have heard authors say that getting an agent is their ultimate goal because they really want a traditional publishing package, but remember that not all agents are created equally. A friend of mine, who did ultimately publish with a Top Five (it was five at the time) New York publisher, wasted a year working with an agent who had reached out to her and said she really wanted to represent her story about organic gardening. A year of closed doors later, my friend had the grit to find a new agent who was able to open more doors. But just like in every other life situation, agents run the gamut; some are great, and some are not.

Why is a traditional publishing contract considered the brass ring in the publishing industry? The author typically receives an advance against royalties (a percentage of book sales) and pays nothing (except for their time) up front to publish. Sounds great. The dirty little secret is that many authors never earn out beyond their advance, meaning that the life of living on passive income to which many authors aspire is a false dream. Later, I will give you some actual data on what traditional publishing advances look like today as well as earn outs.

Other reasons to go with a traditional publisher include that they generally assure distribution to physical bookstores, have great connections to media outlets, and have a team of people with a considerable amount of experience working on every aspect of book publishing—developmental editing, copy editing, proofreading, interior design, cover design, printing, warehousing, distribution, billing, and more. Traditional publishers do not guarantee that your books will sell, of course, and we'll take a look in the following chapter at just how many books the average author can expect to sell.

Also included in the traditional publisher species are smaller or independent presses that still offer many of the same services, usually at a smaller scale. Examples include artistically-oriented publishers like Graywolf and Milkweed or university presses that typically involve peer review and board approval.

SELF-PUBLISHING

I just have to laugh at the descriptor "self" in self-publishing. The process includes so much more than one's self. For my species guide, I will call this category the *entrepreneurial publisher* because you can end up managing a pretty significant team. You need to employ project management skills, assume risk, know how to manage a budget, and much more. Like any entrepreneurial endeavor, if you are successful, the upside is yours to keep.

You'll read soon the results of all of the costs associated with self-publishing, but here is a quick overview of the parts and players that are involved in the "self" publishing process. This is not a comprehensive list, but it shows you that this is not really a one-man or one-woman job, even for those that are most ambitious (or introverted):

- Dealing with logistics, such as getting an ISBN, barcode, and inputting metadata;
- Incorporating a publishing company, unless you use Amazon's CreateSpace, which we'll cover in the next chapter;
- Hiring and managing a developmental editor;
- Hiring and managing a copy editor;
- Hiring and managing a proofreader;
- Hiring and managing an interior (book layout) designer;
- Hiring and managing a cover designer;
- Figuring out how to print and warehouse your book (if you have physical copies);
- Figuring out how to distribute your book;
- Developing and managing your marketing plan, including ads, book reviews, website, and awards; and
- Developing and managing your publicity plan, including guest blogging, articles, radio interviews, podcast interviews, and TV appearances.

All of the above should be done cost-effectively and without driving yourself crazy. I have found that a business degree helps as you try to manage your career as an author, but as long as you step into the "entrepreneurial" role and own it, you have the mind-set you need. You will also definitely benefit from the survival tips covered in Chapter Six.

HYBRID PUBLISHERS

Remember when I was all excited to tell my friends that I was an "author to be" after getting a few offers from publishers? I also mentioned that the integrity of these offers had yet to stand up to the test of time. As I flipped through the pages of these contracts, the wording read almost exactly like the consulting proposals that I used to write back in the days when I sold millions of dollars of consulting work to large companies.

Your needs are ... and our company has the ability to meet those needs.

Our work plan will consist of the following steps and milestones ...

The team we will assign to you will be made up of ...

The costs for the completion of the above will be ...

WHAAAAAAT!?!?!?!?!

The price tags for some of these proposals were also along the lines of what I would charge my corporate clients for months of work.

I called the contact at one of the hybrid publishers that sent me a proposal. His title was Consultant, which should have caught my attention, and he took my call right away. He was articulate and spoke eloquently of the "walls of tears"—books stacked high in his office that were sent to him as pleas for help, the authors overcome with grief that their books had not done well in the marketplace and needed a complete makeover by his publishing company (at the cost of a luxury car, I would learn later). Didn't I want to sign with his firm and avoid those tears? After all, I had gotten as far as only 3% of the authors that reached out to this company. This may have been true; the firm was recommended to me by an industry expert who had no financial gain in sending me their way. I ended up saying no to the big spend. I called him about a month later with a question and never got a call (or email or text, nada) back. I didn't find that very "consultant-like." Remember, I'm a consultant myself; I don't have anything against consultants, and I think that many of them can really provide unprecedented positive change for their clients. Top-notch consultants invest in the long-term relationship (not the quick sale) and should return a phone call or email to people with whom they have a relationship, even if the billing clock is not ticking. If you're poking around the hybrid publishing industry, pay close attention to what people are calling themselves title-wise. Stay alert and be aware that you are dealing with companies and positions that are rapidly evolving.

I am a big gardener, and I love edible plants as well as ornamental flowers. I remember learning in high school science class that you can take a red flower and combine it with a white flower and ... voila! you have a pink hybrid flower. Pink is in the middle of red and white. Then I started to think about what middle ground this species (the consultant I talked to who never called me back) occupies.

Traditional publishers give advances and self-publishing does not. I would expect a middle ground, or hybrid, would logically provide an advance between big and zero. Nope.

Traditional publishers provide all the book development, marketing, and publicity services; whereas with self-publishing, you're on your own. A middle ground, hybrid, would logically be a range of services between full serve and self-serve. Nope. This guy wanted to sell me everything I could possibly afford, from brand messaging to creating ancillary products for my book.

Then it hit me: Hybrid is an inaccurate name for this species. Hybrid publishers are really just *publishing services companies.* Perhaps the only thing that is hybrid about the situation is that the publisher pays for some services (often with money you've given them), and you also pay for some services out of pocket. But I still think that is a silly word for this industry. I would like to stick with "publishing services company" for my species guide.

Okay, so now we have a basic layout of the major species in publishing. To recap, I'll use the words that I think best to describe these species:

1. Traditional publishers = what most people consider publishing but is becoming much less mainstream.
2. Self-publishing = entrepreneurial publishing.
3. Hybrid publishing = using a publishing services company.

Hopefully, I described these creatures without leading you to any conclusion one way or the other as to whether they are harmful or beneficial. They just are what they are, and the more closely you can understand what their role is in this world (and how they might interact with you if you are walking in their world), the better off you will be.

These creatures do not live alone in the wild world of publishing, as evolution is hitting the industry hard. Evolution is necessary so that life can survive in what are some pretty tough conditions. The next chapter will paint the picture of just how harsh the living conditions are in the wild world of publishing and introduce some of the evolution that is already taking place. Let's keep moving ahead on our journey.

CHAPTER 4

Harsh Living Conditions and Evolution

"Sailors fighting in the dance hall. Oh man! Look at those cavemen go. It's the freakiest show."

~ David Bowie

This is the chapter when we pull out the Compass from our backpacks and have it ready in this wild world of publishing. Your compass is somewhat of an internal GPS, allowing you to check in with your gut instincts and intuition so that you don't end up in the bad part of town. You see, when food (profits) gets scarce and there are more and more species moving in to get their share of whatever is left, things can get ugly. Fights break out, people get taken advantage of, tears are shed. Wolves dress as grandmothers. Dear author, let's not leave you in this increasingly dangerous landscape unprepared and unarmed.

MICROECONOMICS 101

Let's start with a basic overview of what we all learned in Microeconomics 101: the law of supply and demand. In a nutshell, when supply goes up and demand goes down, prices plummet. So let's see what has happened in the publishing industry along these two axes.

Supply: Last I checked, we expect two million new books to be published in 2017. There are already around 20 million books to choose from on Amazon on any given day. Situation? Flooded marketplace.

Demand: Data show that nearly 25% of American adults have not read a single book in the past year. The median number of books read by Americans per year is five. So, really, we are not reading a lot of books. Anecdotal conversations with the younger generation have confirmed my suspicions that they are reading a ton of content online but not really hunkering down and reading good old fashion books. Situation? Insufficient demand.

Outcome: Prices of books are plummeting. Whether or not publishers are ready to slash the price they put on a barcode on the back of a book, the perceived value in the market of books is way down.

An example of this plummet in perceived value is the boom in the industry of services that allows authors to deeply discount their e-books or even offer them for free. Authors are taught that in order to raise the awareness of their work, they should run promotions through which the author pays several hundred dollars or more to offer an ebook to readers for 99 cents. I get it. If you pay $500 for this service and 501 people buy your book, you make money—almost a whole dollar. More importantly, people hear about your book. Because of the exposure concept, I did a similar promotion for *Mountain Mantras: Wellness and Life Lessons from the Slopes* through my distributor. Unfortunately, I lost money—it took a lot of ebook sales to hit the number I paid for the service. Amazon's Kindle Direct Publishing (KDP) rewards its members who choose exclusivity with its program for the first 90 days by allowing up to five "free days" (at no charge to the author). I chose this route for *Give It a Go, Eat a Rainbow*, even though I believe that children's books are best consumed the good old fashioned way—in print—but those promotion days brought readers.

The important point is that we are training consumers to value books as they would any item at a dollar store. Many consumers wait until a book is offered for 99 cents (or free) before they bite. The self-publishing-rumor-mill teaches authors that a sweet spot for an e-book is between 99 cents and $2.99. Given that the Author Outreach Survey results showed that my author group spent an average of 1,000 hours creating, marketing, and publicizing their books, their hourly wage calculates out to about $5/hour, much less than if they took a job at McDonald's. It's just the reality of the numbers, which we'll see in much more detail in the next chapter.

THE PORTER ANALYSIS

As a management consultant geek, I like processes and frameworks to analyze things. So I dug out my Harvard Business School case study on Michael Porter's Five Forces analysis to apply it to the publishing industry. The Porter Analysis looks at the competitive atmosphere of an industry based on five forces. The framework analyzes the level of competition within an industry and, therefore, its attractiveness based on profitability. The stronger the forces, the bigger the squeeze on the industry, meaning that profit margins decline and the industry becomes less attractive. The five forces and my take on the publishing industry follow:

1. *Threat of substitute products.* Assessment: **HIGH**. With millions of books on Amazon and other online retailers and volumes stacking up in brick and mortar stores, readers have more to pick and choose from than ever before.

2. *Threat of established rivals.* Assessment: **HIGH**. With the New York publishers continuing to consolidate (I almost can't

keep up), large established publishers with media arms—often inside their own corporate entities—put resources behind publishing projects that few independent publishers can or would want to match.

3. *Threat of new entrants.* Assessment: **HIGH**. You'll read below about the democratization of publishing that has opened the floodgates to a once elite and guarded industry.

4. *Bargaining power of customers.* Assessment: **HIGH.** There are choices everywhere, bargain shopping abounds, and plenty of opportunities to return and resell books to milk their value.

5. Bargaining power of suppliers. Assessment: **MEDIUM.** From the viewpoint of the author and publisher, suppliers include editors, printers, design firms, publicity firms, and other service providers. This area might be the most dynamic, as the industry shifts from offset printing to Print-On-Demand, while confusion in the industry drives up the need for more players, such as book doctors, coaches, shepherds, and others. Predators also move in. I'll discuss predators later in this chapter. Keep your compass out.

Overall assessment: Level of squeeze? I ... can't ... breathe. Level of attractiveness? I'd say it's looking like ... Gollum. Or maybe Jabba the Hut. Either way, the industry might just eat you alive.

THE ECONOMICS OF THE AVERAGE BOOK

According to BookScan, which tracks most bookstore, online, and other retail sales of books, the average U.S. book sells less than 250 copies per year and less than 3,000 copies over its lifetime.

VENTURE CAPITAL

If the average book sells only 250 copies per year, and the books themselves cost thousands of dollars to produce (see actual numbers in the next chapter), how are publishers staying in business? And how are authors putting food on the table?

Good questions. First of all, even the big boy publishers are getting hit. When the New York publishers released their financials for the first half of 2016, it looked like this:

- Penguin Random House: sales down 10.7%
- Hachette Book Group: sales down 6.6%
- Simon & Schuster: sales down 3.5%
- HarperCollins Publishers: sales down 2.5%

I realize that just because sales are down, it does not mean these companies are not profitable, but I can assure you that people are losing their jobs in this environment as costs are cut. I am starting to understand the publishing business as not so much a crap shoot but as a venture capital portfolio.

Here is an over-simplified version of how the venture capital industry works. Take a venture capital portfolio of ten companies: one or two will go out of business altogether, five or six might just barely chug along (dubbed the walking dead), and the entire operation is kept afloat by that heavy hitter or two that hits it big-time. Think IPO and lots of rich, happy investors.

We have just seen that in the publishing industry, the vast majority of books do not earn much money, some lose money, and some knock it out of the park. "Knock it out of the park" means they hit the *New York Times* Best Sellers list (selling in the hundreds of thousands of copies) and make the whole venture worth it for the people who are lucky enough to have that book in their portfolio.

Making it in the venture capital industry—or in the publishing industry—is about volume. You have to have enough companies (or books) in your portfolio to make the numbers work. As an author or a small independent publisher with one, two, or even several books, you are not able to play the numbers game. Outlook for the small publisher or author: Very risky if you are selling books only.

Now, don't be depressed and put this book down already, dear author. In the final chapter on survival, we'll talk about diversification strategies that can help you win. Hang in there.

THE DEMOCRATIZATION OF PUBLISHING

Evolutionary species: Amazon (CreateSpace)

Mention "Amazon" in a group of bookstore owners, and you'll feel as though you've just shouted "Voldemort!" in one of the *Harry Potter* books. Yes, Amazon is probably responsible for mass closings of independent bookstores, some of the big chains like Borders going out of business, and some of the distribution industry giants like Partners deciding to exit after decades in the business, but Amazon is not evil. Amazon is a very, very smart player in a capitalist economy.

I have a friend who owns a bookstore, and she sees people all the time come in, leaf through a book—perhaps sit and read half of it while lounging in one of those comfy book store chairs—and then look it up on Amazon and buy it online. It sends my friend's blood pressure through the roof, but, hopefully, they at least bought a muffin or a cup of coffee while they sat there and read. The fact is, the price of the book on Amazon is likely the price of a muffin or cup of coffee LESS than what they would pay in the store. With free shipping on Amazon Prime, customers get the book pretty quickly, although not immediately. Bookstore owners, Amazon is not going away.

In fact, Amazon is jumping into the brick-and-mortar bookstore business itself, starting with a hometown store in Seattle. Its stores are smaller than a Barnes & Noble (less rent), carry fewer books (lower inventory costs), and have no price tags (they ask people to look up prices on their phones using the Amazon app).

For authors, Amazon has been on the front lines of innovation, as well. Amazon's CreateSpace has been an option for authors since 2009; it allows authors to retain their intellectual property rights, upload files to its system, and utilize Print-On-Demand technology to avoid the significant upfront costs of large offset print runs. Amazon also offers its Kindle KDP service for ebooks, which provides marketing services like the free days I mentioned above. Amazon, through CreateSpace and KDP, has democratized the world of publishing, since anyone can create an account, upload a file, and start selling their written words.

Evolutionary species: Ingram (IngramSpark)

I told the story earlier about how I had originally started my journey with a hybrid publisher that pitched my book cover to Ingram, the wholesaler that dominates the sales channel to bookstores. Ingram is not as fast and technology-focused as Amazon, but it is a darn well-run company, from what I have seen. Year 2013 marked the official launch of IngramSpark, basically the same idea as CreateSpace (author uploads files, retains rights, and prints on demand). IngramSpark has a few other perks, mainly that it can print hardback books—CreateSpace currently does not—and offers access to Ingram's channels to bookstores. But from what I have heard from authors using IngramSpark, your books will not show up in bookstores unless you have a massive campaign across the country asking all of your friends to request the book at the bookstores themselves. Since it will show up in the computer at a bookstore (using Ingram's system which doesn't involve shouting "Voldemort!" as you would with a CreateSpace/Amazon ISBN), the store owner can and may order it. But please remember what I said earlier about bookstore returns.

Other evolutionary species

For e-books, there are other great sources out there, including Smashwords, which can get your ebook into all the ebook channels, such as Nook (Barnes & Noble), iBook (Apple), Kobo, and many others.

WOLVES AND SHEPHERDS

Let's imagine a peaceful farming community with sheep grazing in its spacious yet confined area, all getting enough food. That might have been the publishing industry in the middle of the 20th century. Then the digital age came, the squeeze took hold, and food supply became short as herds of millions of new sheep swept into the countryside and knocked down all the fences that kept everyone and everything in order. It is now quite chaotic, with lost sheep roaming everywhere. Who tends to emerge in such situations?

Wolves

I mentioned that, early in my publishing journey, I felt excluded from the club. Ah, how this feeling changed when I became known as an author in certain circles, especially online. I started getting calls, emails, texts, and pings on social media from all kinds of people who, at first, were huge inflators to my ego—until I realized that they were simply trying to distract me while they got some cash out of my pocket. Here are some of the most egregious players who stalked me, dressed like grandmas and hiding their big white fangs. Fortunately, I caught on early in most cases and guarded my wallet.

- The radio show producer who said I was *such* a great personality that I should have my own show on their network (paying thousands of dollars per year in the process). Huh, I already had a radio show and a podcast that costs me $20 a month on Libsyn.
- The TV producer who said I should appear in an interview with a famous actor to promote my expertise—I am so sad to say that it happened to be one of my favorite fictional heroes from my teens—at a frightening cost of tens of thousands of dollars.
- Vanity presses (a sub-species of publishing services companies) that reached out to me, telling me my books had such

promise to go big-time, especially when I had just done a successful campaign on Kickstarter and had a few grand in my pocket to publish my first children's book, *Give It a Go, Eat a Rainbow*. Notice the correlation between a public forum that anyone can search to find out who has funds (*e.g.*, Kickstarter) and the emergence of folks wanting to stroke my ego?

- Fake literary agents who reached out to me asking for money in order to represent my work to publishers. Note: you do not pay an agent out of your pocket. As in the real estate industry, they get paid when the transaction happens—when they sell your proposal to an editor or publisher.
- Contest scams, in which your work is published in an anthology, yet the only way to get your hands on the finished product is to pay an outrageous fee ($60 to $100 for a book? Ah ... no).

I have an aspiring author friend who has been scammed out of nearly ten thousand dollars. She was told that a company would do everything from incorporate her business to help her raise money to design a beautiful website. Nothing. The owner of the company faked his death (due to a tooth infection, of all things!). The private investigation fees to go after the guy were beyond what my friend wanted to deal with, so she let it go. You'll hear more stories in the next chapter, especially under the questions I posed to my author friends: What is the most bizarre thing about the publishing industry, and what was the WORST money you spent in the publishing industry? The answers might make you laugh or cry, but they are meant to allow you to use your compass and avoid the wolves before they sniff YOU out first and attempt to lure you in.

Shepherds

You don't have to be eaten alive by the big bad wolf. There are some honest, good people who have stepped up in the industry to help aspiring authors stay clear of the bad guys. Some of them literally call themselves book shepherds, some are book coaches, some are book doctors, and some are business coaches, who also have lots of experience in the publishing industry. Yes, most charge a fee for their time, but the idea is that you will end up saving a lot of time and money by having someone explain the process to you. They are guides and usually serve entrepreneurial publishers, and they hold your hand through every decision you make.

There are also group book coaching programs in which you go through the process with a cohort as well as online group courses you can take. A couple of examples that I have been a part of myself include the Bestseller Blueprint by Jack Canfield and Steve Harrison as well as Self Publishing School by Chandler Bolt. I am a big believer in ongoing education, and even though I am a coach myself, I also hire coaches who can help me jump to the next level.

In addition, I highly recommend joining an author, writer, and/or publisher group (nonprofit or industry association) that will provide you with access to trusted industry insiders and lots of insider resources, which will also save you tons of time and money. I am on the Benefits Committee of the Independent Book Publishers Association and have found my home within this group, a nice thing anytime you are feeling like you need a little group support.

Whichever way you decide to build your team, don't wander alone in this squeezed, risky, potentially dangerous world for too long. There is safety in numbers, so find your herd, tribe, or family and build your own protection for the sake of your wallet and your sanity.

Now, it's time for some real insight into the stories and numbers of authors in my own personal network. The next chapter provides you with the nitty gritty on what it can cost to develop, print, market, and publicize a book, along with the investments of time across all of these areas. We'll learn about goals and hear short stories about some of the best and worst moments. Strap yourself in for an emotional ride ...

CHAPTER 5

Reality

"I was brought to my senses;
I was blind but now that I can see ..."

~ **Sting**

This chapter will share the current reality from the trenches of the publishing industry. I'll share with you the real, and often hilarious and heartbreaking, feedback from a set of brave authors who bared their financial souls and truths in the Author Outreach Survey that I conducted with several dozen writers across traditional, self, and hybrid publishing methods. I don't consider these results to be scientifically blessed (*e.g.*, significant sample size, double blind, placebo). I didn't spam thousands of people and author groups all over the web to find participants.

Instead, I hand selected and invited a cozy group of folks who I knew would be honest and take the time to fill out what ended up being a hearty, deep-dive set of questions designed to uncover some key messages. I have conducted and analyzed lots of surveys as part of my prior work in management consulting and still do surveys for clients today, so I know the power of a well-designed survey and the importance of a network of people who care enough to fill it out honestly and thoroughly.

In fact, as I started to reach out to author friends to gauge their interest in participating, I noticed that many were feeling just a little anxious about looking at the financial side of their projects. One of my author friends said, "It might be too painful to complete. Writing a book is like raising a child. The ROI [return on investment] is hard to equate to dollars and cents. Throwing good money after a risky venture is usually an act of love".

It was indeed an act of love for these brave souls to participate in the survey, and you'll see the care in the responses that are aimed at helping new (and experienced) authors learn what to expect before they jump in with both feet.

Some authors, even those I know well, just couldn't muster the desire to participate; some were simply too busy to meet the deadline. One book coach who had published with an infamous hybrid publisher (*aka* publishing services company) said to me, "This is a great project, but you are potentially uncovering the publishing industry's deep, dark secret [that there is little money to be made in publishing for most people]."

Deep, dark secret? I'm not sure that any of the responses were much of a surprise to me, as I have heard a lot of crazy stories and have been active in the publishing industry for years.

I asked for dollar figures in ranges, not exact amounts, because I know that many authors struggle with accounting systems—either their publisher's, distributor's, or self-managed spreadsheets. The survey was organized in eight sections, as follows:

1. Goals and background
2. Book development
3. Book printing
4. Book distribution
5. Book marketing
6. Book publicity
7. Time
8. Short stories

You can get the complete, nitty gritty survey report at www.makewellnessfun.com/authorsurvey. In that downloadable PDF, you'll see every comment made as well as summary charts. This chapter simply covers the highlights across the three types of publishing: Traditional, Self, and Hybrid.

TRADITIONAL PUBLISHER SURVEY HIGHLIGHTS

These are my friends who got the brass ring (or so they thought) in the publishing industry by signing a traditional publishing contract. Interestingly, in most cases, publishers approached these authors, rather than the other way around. At least in my survey sample, the idea that you must have an agent to get a traditional publishing deal was myth-busted; less than one-third of the authors surveyed used an agent. Fifty-seven percent of the authors had multiple books, and 43% were first-time authors. Reasons for pursuing the traditional publishing route included:

- "I have a Ph.D. in creative writing, and traditional publication is the expected path at this level."
- "I wanted to have access to indie bookstores, libraries, magazine and newspaper book reviewers, and PR."
- "More credibility in my field."

As far as meeting goals related to their books, this group was less enthusiastic than the self-published group of authors you'll soon meet. Traditional authors scored the lowest in terms of their "achievement to goal" at 3.3 and 3.0 (average and median), although not extremely behind the happiest group (self-published authors), who reported scores of 3.5 and 4.0 (average and median) out of 5.0. Disappointment among traditionally published authors centered around issues such as publishers not living up to the authors' expectations.

In several severe cases, the publisher had gone out of business, leaving the author scrambling to buy up inventory and find new distribution. I also heard about a publisher who did not distribute on Amazon, so the author had to buy back the e-book rights to distribute on Amazon Kindle Direct Publishing.

Getting stuck in a contract with unfavorable terms was a big risk factor for both traditionally and hybrid-published authors. Self-published authors, as author-entrepreneurs, avoided this potential pitfall.

It was interesting to learn from the survey that traditionally published authors actually spent the *most* time of all groups developing their books, despite having the support of their traditional publishing partners.

Show me the money

The real—perceived—brass ring in a traditional publishing deal is the author advance. But here, the shine is not as bright as one might think. More than 40% of surveyed authors did not receive any advance at all, another 30% received an advance that was less than $5,000, and the remaining 30% received more. The rare author receiving an advance near the six-digit mark spent hefty sums on proposal development (~$10,000) and paid for ghostwriting services out of pocket (~$25,000). In fact, more than half of the traditionally published authors incurred costs to prepare their proposals, and all amounts were in excess of $2,500. All of the traditionally published authors also invested in a team outside of their publisher's team, ranging from executive assistants and virtual assistants to coaches and book marketing advisors. Traditionally published authors made comments such as, "The authors make so little," despite the fact that all of the traditionally published books recorded sales in excess of 500 copies, with more than 40% selling over 5,000 copies.

Most traditional publishers paid for reviews, but few paid for ads or giveaways. No traditional publishers created a website for the author or book as part of the publishing contract. Over 70% of the traditional publishers provided a publicist as part of the contract, but authors made comments such as, "My publisher didn't get me all of the prominent media that I wanted, so I ended up getting some of it myself." More money was spent overall on publicity for traditionally published books, averaging several thousand dollars per book and in excess of $15,000 for some books. Three quarters of traditionally published authors were not satisfied with the services provided by the publishers' publicists. Further, all traditionally published authors who paid for a publicist out of pocket said that this money for publicity was "not a good spend."

Winner for the most hilarious comment

"Hahahaha! It is all bizarre! It doesn't work the way people think it does—publishing and marketing are FAR more hands-on than anyone thinks."

Winner for the most heartbreaking comment

"We do all the work, and they take all the money and don't bother to market their own published books. No real training about what to expect or how best to prepare for launch."

Advice for aspiring authors from traditionally published authors

- "GET HELP! This isn't a world to try to understand by yourself. Hire experienced people to help you all along the way and learn how to maximize your impact."
- "Prepare your own PR campaign and expect nothing from your publisher. Begin the process six months before launch. Get a social network and Twitter following before the book is out."
- "Publishing is a complicated industry, and Amazon is definitely the easiest and cheapest way to get started. If you have other goals, like being a *New York Times* bestseller or getting into bookstores or libraries, be sure to speak to someone who has actually done it recently for the type of book you write."
- "Be careful negotiating the contract—find out all you can about using a traditional publisher before you sign."

SELF-PUBLISHER SURVEY HIGHLIGHTS

First, let me tell you a little bit about this group. The majority of the authors were first-time authors (62%), with the remaining 38% having already published multiple books. One of the authors already had twelve books published, plus a reported stack of manuscripts, so don't get the impression that this group was inexperienced in the writing world. Three-quarters of the authors looked into other methods of publishing: either traditional, hybrid, or both. Others beelined straight to self-publishing and cited the following reasons:

- Desire for fast speed to market, given time-sensitive subject matter.
- Lack of contacts in the publishing industry.
- Hearsay from traditionally published authors that the bulk of the work still rests on the authors (platform building, marketing, promotion), so why give away most of the revenue on book sales?
- Desire to maintain control over the message, product, and brand.

As far as meeting the goals related to their books, this group is a pretty happy bunch overall. More than half of the authors exceeded their goals, 38% met their goals, and only 6% felt they underachieved. The disappointed minority generally had goals along the lines of broad reach and impact, perhaps harder to accomplish from a self-published platform. The desire to get a message out resonated in nearly every survey response; perhaps expectations of how far the message would carry are correlated to ultimate satisfaction.

Examples of goals that echoed throughout the group include:

- Achieving expert status;
- Sharing a story that others can benefit from and change their lives; and
- Enjoyment of writing and the creative process.

Show me the money

Self-published authors in the survey were true to the statistics previously quoted regarding average book sales; nearly two-thirds of survey participants reported sales of less than 500 copies, with the balance selling less than 2,500 copies. The good news is that all of the authors in this group used POD services, meaning that these folks did not have to invest a significant cash outlay for an offset print run. In contrast, in the traditionally published group, 86% of the books were printed using offset printing, meaning the publisher paid thousands of dollars upfront to get the books ready for distribution. Self-published authors did, however, spend quite a bit of money to get their books produced, including logistical setups, such as ISBN and POD setup, editing, interior layout, cover design, etc. Interestingly, and likely due to the fact that so much of the budget was spent on book development, self-published authors spent *considerably* less money on book marketing and publicity than traditionally and hybrid published authors. The large discrepancy in amounts spent on marketing and publicity (with self-published authors spending a quarter to half of the amount spent by traditional and hybrid published authors, respectively) likely accounts for the lackluster sales of self-published books. All of the detailed numbers are available at www.makewellnessfun.com/authorsurvey.

Self-published authors spent approximately 300 days developing their books, about 20% longer than the hybrid published authors but faster than traditionally published authors.

Winner for the most hilarious comment

"There are more people who would like to write a book than read a book."

Winner for the most heartbreaking comment

"Every minute of every day, my book haunts me."

Advice for aspiring authors from the self-published crowd

- "Only write what you love, otherwise you are wasting your time."
- "There are countless paths to success, take each piece of advice with a grain of salt."

- "Be patient. Create a good quality book. Have fun but also treat your business seriously."
- "Go for it!!!!! You are enough! You know enough! People need what you know and can help them with. Here's a wonderful story that I'll never forget: After I had published my book and been out there promoting it, I started getting calls with people saying, "We're looking for someone to come speak to our organization. We're looking for the expert. We see you've authored a book. We want you." They weren't looking for anyone else, not tire-kicking. I was the expert because I'd published the book. The best way to catapult your expert status and business growth is to write your book. DO it!!!"

HYBRID PUBLISHER SURVEY HIGHLIGHTS

Hybrid authors, or those who used a publishing services company to bring their books to life, were a group very true to the word "hybrid." Their happiness with the journey was *all over the board.* The huge range in satisfaction is not surprising, given that there are so many different companies calling themselves hybrid publishers and accepting money in exchange for various, sometimes ill-defined, services. Authors in this group chose the publishing services route for reasons such as:

- Fear of self-publishing due to lack of knowledge in the publishing industry,

- Not being able to gain attention of traditional publishers without a literary agent, and
- The idea that they (the hybrid publisher) would take care of a lot of the details—formatting, ISBN, etc.

Goals for publishing for this group of authors mirrored the goals of traditionally and self-published authors and centered around the ideas of spreading valuable messages, helping people, and advancing expert status. Author satisfaction with achievement to goals was slightly below that of self-published authors and about on par with traditionally published authors. The comments from the hybrid published authors were without question the most passionate, as these individuals were often locked into contracts that they were pleased with or felt very trapped in.

Show me the money

Just less than half of surveyed authors in the hybrid publishing group reported offset printing their books, averaging 1,300 copies printed initially. Approximately 70% reported sales of less than 500 copies overall, while 30% reported selling more than 5,000 copies. On average, authors in this segment sold approximately 3,000 copies, more than three times their self-published peers. These numbers are possibly inflated by the fact that a number of hybrid publishers include an obligatory buy-out of books by the author, often up to several thousand copies.

Those surveyed said contracts with hybrid publishers, which generally cover book development, marketing, (limited) publicity, and, in most cases, printing, distribution, warehousing, etc., ran the gamut from a couple thousand dollars to nearly $10,000 upfront. I've personally seen contracts that cost up to $60,000 plus a share of the royalties and other back-end services.

In general, hybrid-published authors paid less overall (roughly half) to develop their books than self-published authors but considerably more on marketing and publicity (more than four times). Perhaps hybrid publishing firms are more experienced in developing books cost-effectively than self-published authors who have to assemble a team of outside vendors. Another likely possibility is that self-published authors spend their budgets, knowingly or not, on developing their books and have little left for marketing and publicity. Hybrid-published authors spent on average another $7,750 out of pocket on marketing and publicity in addition to their contracts with publishers. Again, all of the detailed numbers are available at www.makewellnessfun.com/authorsurvey.

Hybrid-published authors took slightly less time than self-published authors to develop their books, averaging 250 days as compared to 300 days for self-published authors.

Winner for the most hilarious comment

"People think they will make a lot of money on their books, but truth be told, unless you are a starlet, politician, or total pervert, you probably won't make much money. Instead, focus on helping people with your message."

Winner for the most heartbreaking comment (it was a tie)

- "I hate the way that many publishers prey on uninformed writers trying to become published. They produce poor quality books, often unedited, with poor covers, with excessive up-front costs, and more negative stuff. In spite of warnings from friends, agents, other publishers, and experienced authors, many fall into this trap."
- "[The worst part about the publishing industry is] the lack of integrity and professionalism. Once the publisher gets you in, they don't support you and just want you to pay more money in their marketing scams. Also, they will try to lock you in with a contract so you can't even write another book unless you give them first right of refusal. That's unconscionable!"

Advice for aspiring authors from hybrid authors

- "First, write the best book you can. Then, take your time, do your homework and learn as much as you can about the publishing industry, book design and formatting, marketing, and publicity—then make informed and intelligent decisions."

- "Focus on why you are writing the book. Who is your audience? What do you want them to feel? Do? Become? Don't focus on making money and don't spend too much money on the publishers' marketing scams. Do your own marketing through social media and try to get out and share your message by doing presentations and speeches. Then, you can have your book available for sale. Don't depend on any publisher to do anything they say they are going to do. Too many of them are all about volume and not at all about quality. And even though they say they care about their authors, unfortunately, that's usually not the case. Also, realize that there are critics out there who will write awful reviews just because they can. Don't let them discourage you from getting your message out there. Remember that you can't please all of the people all of the time. Keep writing from the heart because you love it!"
- "Be aware that it's not easy to market and publicize a book—but if you have a book that needs to be written, write it anyway! There is a lot of self-satisfaction in seeing your own book become real."

Now that you have a picture of the reality of the wild world of publishing, we'll dive right in to the strategies that you can follow to THRIVE, not just survive, on your author journey.

CHAPTER 6

Survival of the Fittest (and That Means YOU)

"Work is fun!"

~ **Will Ferrell in the movie** *Elf*

'WHY' IS YOUR WEAPON

No matter what type of publishing method you use to get your book out into the world, you must always rely on the "why" of your writing and career as an author. I can't possibly come up with all the reasons you might want to be an author, but I'll pick the top three that came up again and again in my Author Outreach Survey and give you customized advice for each. You'll still need your Map, Bug Spray, Species Guide, and

Compass. These survival tips will make sure that you rise to the top of the evolutionary pack and don't get eaten alive. In fact, my hope is that you have some fun and adventure along the way. Most importantly, I want your monthly reviews of your income statements to be peaceful and pleasant (not painful) experiences.

WHY? BECAUSE YOU WANT A CREATIVE OUTLET

General advice: Do not place any pressure on your writing to sustain yourself financially. Ah, doesn't that already feel good? Think about your writing as a hobby. Consider the time you spend writing as an alternative to time spent gardening, knitting, cooking, baking, making videos, painting, decorating, restoring old cars, or WHATEVER makes you happy in your free time; anyone writing a book in order to leave a legacy would fall into this category. These types of activities allow you to live a creative life; and most of them actually cost money to pursue. Gardeners need to buy tools, fertilizer, soil, and seeds, and they spend lots of time nurturing those pretty little plants. I have yet to see a plant-lover walk into their garden and start scolding the flowers, "Where's my return on investment!? Why aren't you producing more blooms and blossoms!?" A gardener simply notices the results of his or her work and treats the creative project with gentle hands and curiosity. If you write as a means of expressing your creativity or as a hobby, I suggest you enjoy it as such.

Advice for financial success: All hobbies should be kept to a budget, however, so create a budget for your writing and your book projects, too. Look at the detailed numbers in the self-publishing and hybrid (*aka* publishing services) surveys and decide whether you are going to go high-end or low-end. For information about an amazing, cutting edge tool that allows you to organize and record text, images, video, and audio so you can have the most fun with your creative adventure, see my blog post www.makewellnessfun.com/creativewriter.

Hire your dog or cat to be your marketing director and tell them, "No ads—bad dog, bad kitty!" if they approve any budget beyond electronic ads or social media. Don't hire a high-priced publicist, but go ahead and learn about podcasts and other cost-effective ways to highlight your value and work. Or join an author community. For more ideas, see www.makewellnessfun.com/authorcommunities.

If you want a physical copy of your book in your hands, use POD through CreateSpace and/or Ingram Spark. For trusted helping hands, please see www.makewellnessfun.com/authorresources.

Advice for time management: Have fun writing your book. Be proud of it. If things are going well in writer/creator land, imagine yourself as an elf, just like Will Ferrell when he says, "Smiling's my favorite!" Stop your work when you get annoyed or when you find you are ignoring your day job. As with the garden, if the weeds take over from neglect, that's an indication that it's time to pursue a different hobby.

If you have so much fun with your first book that you want to do another, by all means continue. Treat your creative writing hobby as you would a beloved garden that you have cultivated: plan, seed, water, give tons of light, nurture, and give lots of TLC. Enjoy it as you bask in its beauty. Invite others to visit your garden, but don't be offended if they have a preference for other types of colors, aromas, or arrangements or don't like gardening at all. If you love your creative outcome, that's really all that matters.

WHY? BECAUSE YOU WANT TO ADVANCE YOUR CAREER AND STATUS AS AN EXPERT

General advice: Write a book that can serve as a high-end, high-value business card for where you want your professional life to go. If you already have a steady source of income otherwise and want to increase it, you may see writing a book as a promising next step in that process. However, like the gardener, you'll need to get over the fact that your book is unlikely to make you any money by itself. Go out and pick up a copy of Elizabeth's Gilbert's *Big Magic* and underline all the parts about how she took a pledge that she would never put pressure on her writing to support herself financially. Then, review these parts periodically, just in case you start to get wild dreams about million dollar royalty checks. Create an understanding with yourself that if you never make money from your writing, that will be okay. After all, you haven't left your day job, and your writing is more of a side hustle or a tool for your professional advancement.

Make your book look as professional as possible. Avoid the top six biggest giveaways that scream, "This book was not produced by a high-end publisher":

1. Typos;
2. Formatting mistakes;
3. Unappealing cover;
4. CreateSpace ISBN (Sorry, Amazon, I love you, but most bookstores do not);
5. No logo on the spine; and
6. Barcode that does not show the book's price.

Unless you are worried about self-publishing snobbery, maybe you don't care about the last three points. But, by all means, take care of the first three!

If your book is a business card for your money-making projects, it should employ strategies that bring people into your world so that they can get to know, like, and trust you. Have links on the back cover, in the first several pages, and throughout the book that drive people to your website so that you can capture their information and start an ongoing conversation with them. The reason to have links on the back cover and in the first couple of pages of the book (which can be seen via the "Look Inside" feature on Amazon) is that people don't even have to buy your book for you to invite them to your website and capture their email information. You obviously need email management software on your website, and I'd also suggest that you put an electronic lead management tool in place as part of your marketing machine. As new and better products are constantly coming to market, I'm keeping an updated list at www.makewellnessfun.com/websiteresources.

Advice for financial success: You're writing this book for all the good stuff that will happen on the back end, right? So, be sure to have your plan in place to monetize your expert status in the form of speaking fees, courses, coaching, consulting, and product sales. Remember, you're not expecting to earn a lot from book sales, or even earn your money back in most cases, and you still want to have a chunk of your budget left over for ongoing marketing and publicity. Create a total budget that encompasses book development costs (*e.g.*, logistics, editing, interior design, cover design), distribution costs, and POD printing (for physical copies) and still leaves sufficient funds for marketing and publicity. And, lest I forget the incredibly obvious, make sure that when your book comes out, you have already put in place the email and contact management software (which costs money) and created or budgeted for the creation of all of the products and services that will be part of your upsell process.

Learn about how to incorporate CTAs (Calls to Action) in your book, website, and all communication with your audience. You will need to embrace your role—one of many—as Chief Marketing Officer.

The #1 financial mistake authors revealed in the self-published Author Outreach Survey was spending so much of their budget on book development that little was left over for marketing and publicity. I have hosted several webinars specifically for authors about how to get publicity on a budget for their books. You can access these free video training sessions at www.makewellnessfun.com/authorpublicity.

Advice for time management: Write your book as efficiently as possible. Budget a certain amount of time and assign it an opportunity cost (compared to what you would be working on otherwise). If you make $200 an hour coaching, it is helpful to do the math on how much the opportunity cost is if you spend 60 hours writing your book (an opportunity cost of $12,000) vs. 150 hours (an opportunity cost of $30,000). You can write a good book in either amount of time, and I personally would rather incur a $12K opportunity cost rather than a $30K cost. Remember Parkinson's Law which states that a task will expand to the amount of time given to it. Set your timer and get focused. For information about how to cut down your writing time using software specifically designed to nip writer's block in the bud, see my blog post at www.makewellnessfun.com/efficientwriter.

WHY? BECAUSE YOU WANT TO BE AN INFORMATION ENTREPRENEUR

General advice: Follow all the advice for Book as a Business Card and take it to the next level. You want the book to have the highest status possible, and there is nothing better than being able to put "#1 Bestseller" in the same sentence as your book. With the right knowledge about how Amazon works and a launch team, you can achieve this status for your own book. I know because I've done it multiple times. Learn more about the bestseller launch strategy at www.makewellnessfun.com/bestsellerlaunch.

Make sure you have a high degree of social proof around your book and its launch. That means getting at least 25 reviews on Amazon in the first week after launch and at least 100 reviews within several months. Get your book on Goodreads or hire someone to do it for you. Apply for awards and tag on "Award-Winning" to your name and your book the minute you receive one. More information about reviews, awards, and other social proof can be found at www.makewellnessfun.com/authorsocialproof.

Advice for financial success: If you plan on making a living as an infopreneur, you need to have a full escalation model of products, from low-end tripwire products (I typically include a book in this category) all the way up through courses and high-end, live events that may be priced in the five or even six digits. Budget in as many platform-building activities as possible, including social media, blogging, membership communities, speaking, podcasting, guest podcasting, and perhaps even good old fashioned traditional media like radio and TV. Take a look at folks like John Lee Dumas (JLD) who has launched six-figure Kickstarter campaigns around his books (in his case, the *Freedom Journal* in 2016 and the *Mastery Journal* in 2017, both of which I supported). Be prepared to spend money in order to make money. JLD posts his monthly income statements online at www.EOFire.com, if you'd like to get a sense of how much of an investment over time it takes to create an online empire.

Advice for time management: Don't underestimate the amount of time it will take to run your infopreneur business. Plan for anywhere between four and ten hours of time spent on marketing and publicity for each single hour of time spent on content creation. That's right. If it takes you 30 hours to write your book, you should plan up to 300 hours for marketing and publicity. The most efficient use of time I can think of would be to star on 300 high-quality podcasts to promote your work. Use the Pomodoro technique of setting a timer for focused use of time followed by shorter recovery periods. The *Mastery Journal* is a great resource for mastering your productivity, focus, and discipline, all of which you will need to succeed in a world where it is increasingly harder to get noticed among the distractions and noise of the online world.

You will also need a team. If delegation is not a skill you possess today, plan on learning it.

This advice is not meant to be discouraging. In addition to helping people and making a difference in the world, writing a book can get you started on a new trajectory in life, open new doors, and create new opportunities that could indeed be profitable in both the short and long term. Strategy and planning are essential, not optional.

NO MATTER WHAT YOUR WHY, BEWARE OF THE WOLVES

Here is a quick list that will ensure that you are watching your back and checking in with your gut instincts (compass) at all times:

- If it sounds too good to be true, it probably is;
- If the payment terms are 100% upfront, walk away;
- When you are unable to speak with previous clients to get a reference on a service or resource, walk away;
- If a service provider found you on the Internet or social media and you are unable to get any six degree connection with someone you know, proceed only with great caution; and
- Don't sign a contract without having a real attorney review it first. The legal costs of a contract review are much less than the legal costs of fighting to get out of a contract you've already signed.

I'll maintain a list of resources with helpful organizations, groups, and alerts on scams at www.makewellnessfun.com/authorcompass.

Also, just like EOFire's income statements, I've also provided an income statement about the revenues and costs associated with this book, which will be updated monthly. So you can either laugh at my losses or cheer for my wins. Haha or hehe. We'll see!

www.makewellnessfun.com/LBYLIncomeStatements

I wish you the very best with your own writing journey and adventure. Please stay in touch!

Kathryn

ACKNOWLEDGMENTS

It is with great delight that I take this opportunity to express my gratitude for so many individuals and groups who have helped me on this journey. Writing a book is similar to the many other creative processes in my life, one based on collaboration and teamwork.

Within these pages, I've shared with you the stories of many authors who have made a profound difference in my life and have contributed to the book's content and creation. To each of you, I will always be grateful for your contributions and support. I keep a list of names and organizations at www.makewellnessfun.com /lookbeforeyouleapacknowledgements

I also want to thank my family and extended family for being so amazing. Thank you for reminding me to "keep it fun," which is consistent with my brands: *Make Wellness Fun*, *Make Nutrition Fun*, *Make Publishing Fun* and all the other areas in which I intend to put a little more fun in the future.

March 2017

ABOUT THE AUTHOR

KATHRYN KEMP GUYLAY is a speaker, certified nutritional counselor and coach with a master's degree in business administration (MBA).

Kathryn was named a 2016 "Woman of the Year" by the National Association of Professional Women.

The award-winning and bestselling author of four books, she now helps other authors as an author consultant and is the founder of the **Make Publishing Fun** learning academy.

As a sought-after wellness and business expert, Kathryn is often interviewed by leading media such as ABC, CBS, and NPR and hosts two podcasts*: Mountain Mantras: Wellness and Life Lessons* and *Positive on Publishing.*

Kathryn's books to date include:

- *Mountain Mantras: Wellness and Life Lessons from the Slopes*
- *Give It a Go, Eat a Rainbow*
- *Where Does a Rainbow Grow?*
- *Look Before You Leap: The Smart Author's Guide to Avoiding the Money Pit and Achieving Financial SUCCESS in Publishing*

More information about Kathryn's products and services can be found on the following pages.

For more information about Kathryn, please visit www.makewellnessfun.com.

Invite Kathryn to Speak or Be Your Coach

- Need an engaging speaker for your next event?
- Looking for a facilitator who can hold the space with C-Suite executives but also has a heart-centered, warm approach that will leave attendees feeling positive and energized?

You need an expert like Kathryn Kemp Guylay (MBA, CNC) whose 25+ years of experience spans business engagements from small nonprofits to Fortune 500/100 companies. Her speaking and coaching topics and areas of expertise span strategy, organization structure, job definition, incentive plan design, employee engagement, and employee wellness.

To find out how you can book Kathryn in person or via virtual presentations (easy to book through Geniecast speaker services), please visit: www.makewellnessfun.com/speaking

"Kathryn's facilitation at out recent staff retreat made it our best event in years."

—Participant, Annual Staff Retreat at the College of Idaho

Engage with Kathryn at Make Wellness Fun

- Get the latest updates via blog posts and newsletters about productivity, wellness and happiness.
- Benefit from Kathryn's experience and resources as an entrepreneur, helping tens of thousands of people improve their health and wellness.

Make Wellness Fun is the hub for Kathryn's blog posts and resources about wellness and life balance. She weaves experience as a successful entrepreneur, including creating a vision and strategy for life success, with advice for **optimal health and wellness** in your life. Kathryn's goal is to help her readers maximize **productivity and success** across many areas of life.

Learn more at: www.makewellnessfun.com

"Kathryn is a* national leader *for her work to create better health in our nation."

—Dr. David Holmes, Head of School Emeritus; executive director of Strategic Initiatives at Community School of Sun Valley, Idaho

Join Other Aspiring Authors at Make Publishing Fun

- Are you an aspiring author?
- Want to make this world a better place with your advice and knowledge?
- Looking for a supportive community to allow you to bring your book to life?

Whether you suffer from writer's block, don't know where to start, or simply want a community to help you with your journey, I'm here to help.

Make Publishing Fun is an online academy that offers folks like you support in writing, publishing, and marketing books.

Yes, at MPF, our mission is to *Make Publishing Fun.*

Contact me about my special introductory offer at Kathryn@guylay.com. Just say you read about the offer in *Look Before You Leap*, and you can start viewing sample resources for free.

***"The way I would describe Kathryn is* relentlessly helpful."**

—Chrissie Huss, President and Founder of Edible by Design

Listen to Kathryn on her podcasts

The ***Mountain Mantras: Wellness and Life Lessons*** Podcast features today's leaders in the wellness industry as well as successful entrepreneurs and business visionaries. Each show highlights a mantra or set of mantras that listeners can follow and integrate into their days to reach greater heights in their careers and personal lives.

Let the ***Mountain Mantras: Wellness and Life Lessons*** Podcast inspire you to reach for your dreams in wellness, life, and business success. www.makewellnessfun.com/mountainmantraspodcast

The ***Positive on Publishing*** Podcast features published authors and their stories about writing and the creative process. We cover book development, editing, distribution, and marketing for a complete perspective on the journey to bring a book to life. Each show highlights inspirational messages and positive advice for aspiring authors.

Let the ***Positive on Publishing*** Podcast inspire you to transition from aspiring author to published author. www.makewellnessfun.com/positiveonpublishingpodcast

never set foot on the slopes. You'll learn simple ways to make wellness fun.

When you read *Mountain Mantras*, you will learn to:

- **Achieve greater success** in life simply by adjusting how you perceive events around you;
- Discover a six-step framework you can use to **overcome obstacles** in your own life;
- Use **vision and visualization** to turn your dreams into reality; and
- Learn strategies to **engage fully in life,** while experiencing improved health and vitality.

"As a devoted advocate for lifestyle as medicine and an ardent, lifelong skier—this book beautifully conjoins two of my passions. There is expert guidance through the bumps here—with wisdom, experience, and humor on abundant display—and the turns, all well carved. Skiers and eaters will find this an empowering, illuminating read."

—Dr. David Katz, co-founder of Yale University Prevention Research Center and author of *Disease Proof*

To learn more, visit: www.mountainmantras.com

Giving Back

In the spirit of giving back, I am delighted to donate a portion of the proceeds from *Look Before You Leap* to provide scholarships to the learning academies under the umbrella of Make Wellness Fun.

Perhaps you have received this book as a gift or through a free offer or just feel that you have gotten more value than you bargained for in all of the freebies associated with this book. If so, I invite you to make a donation to the 501(c)3 nonprofit for which I volunteer: Nurture.

Nurture is a nonprofit organization dedicated to improving the health and nutrition of children and families. Nurture delivers nutrition and wellness education in a fun, hands-on way with the goal of enhancing the quality of life in our world. Nurture believes that education is an important key in solving health issues plaguing our nation.

Giving back feels good, and giving is one of the pillars of a healthy and full life.

If you feel compelled to make a donation to a worthwhile cause, please go to Nurture's donation link.

www.nurtureyourfamily.org/legacy

NURTURE

www.nurtureyourfamily.org

Thank You For Reading this Book!

I really appreciate your feedback, and I love hearing what you have to say.

Please leave me a helpful review on Amazon letting me know what you think of the book. Just go to Amazon.com and type in “Look Before You Leap”. When you scroll down to the reviews section, there is a grey box (Write a customer review) that you can click on to share your thoughts. Thank you!

P.S. If you haven’t already, don’t forget to grab your free PDF download of the results of the Author Outreach Survey. I look forward to being in touch.

www.makewellnessfun.com/authorsurvey

Made in United States
North Haven, CT
04 November 2026

21765291R00062